A unique collection of three dozen uplifting homilies . . . offers comfort and guidance in coping with the trials of daily life.

—*Brighton Park* and *McKinley Park Life*,
Chicago, IL

I like your book very much. I read it at night. My mother and father also enjoy it greatly.

—Dan Rowan, M.D., Cardiologist,
Little Company of Mary Hospital

Terrific book—I really mean it! I read one story every night. Reminds me of my book.

—Father Tom Hosty, Missionary,
Author of *Straight from the Shoulder*

I predict it will be a best-seller. Congratulations on an excellent book.

—Father George Clements,
President and founder of
One Church, One Addict/One Church, One Child

. . . a collection of 37 homilies delivered over the years in the unusual surroundings of an airport chapel . . . . They're ideas and sentiments that McKenna hopes will have relevance regardless of a person's faith or religious beliefs.

—Sheila Elliott,
Southwest News-Herald, Chicago, IL

I'LL ONLY SPEAK FOR 3 MINUTES

VOLUME 2

I'LL ONLY SPEAK FOR 3 MINUTES

VOLUME 2

More Spiritual Inspirations That Will Change Your Life!

FATHER GEORGE MCKENNA

VEDIC CULTURAL ASSOCIATION PUBLISHING
Honolulu • Los Angeles • Chicago

I'll Only Speak for 3 Minutes, Volume 2
Vedic Cultural Association Publishing / April 1999

Book design by Symes Production & Design
Design concept by Joseph P. Higgins, James E. Higgins III, Judith Higgins Gilbert

Cover Photo by Carrie Leubben
Debra Bragg, Manager

Printed in the United States of America

ISBN 0-89213-248-5

To all the
Chicago Midway Airport
Chapel Volunteer Workers,
past and present,
for their enthusiastic help
and complete dedication.

Contents

Introduction

I first met Father McKenna while attending Quigley Preparatory Seminary South. All the seminarians loved Father for his kindness, humility and wisdom. Twenty-five years and many, many travels later, I began visiting Chicago frequently while working on a book about my life as an astrologer to multi-billionaire Doris Duke. I would often attend Mass at the airport chapel with my mother, Marie. There I met Father McKenna once again.

One day, as Father started his homily with the words, "I will only speak for three minutes," I had a flash of divine inspiration. "That's a book," I exclaimed to myself. I mentioned this to my mother, brother and sister. They all loved the idea. We then approached Father, who enthusiastically embraced the concept. In fact, he had always wanted to publish, but had no idea how to go about it. I assured him that we could do it.

I assembled a competent crew to design and produce the book. In September 1998, after months of working feverishly, volume one of *I'll Only Speak for 3 Minutes* was now available. We had done it. The books sold like hotcakes. People were buying multiple copies and giving them to friends and relatives. The Mayor got a copy. The Cardinal received a copy. Rave reviews came in from everywhere. By January 1999 we were almost out of books and needed to reprint. Based on such a favorable response we are presenting volume two of *I'll Only Speak for 3 Minutes* to provide more of Father

McKenna's insights, inspirations, and love.

What follows is the amazing story of how Father started the chapel at Midway Airport and 36 of his famous three-minute homilies. Enjoy yourself and God bless.

—James E. Higgins III

The Inside Story of Midway Chapel

One cold January day, while sitting in the terminal of Midway Airport, I said to myself, "Wouldn't it be a good thing if religious services could be held somewhere here. It is now January, 1987, and not one religious service has been held at the airport since its opening in 1927."

I put this possibility before Padre Pio, whom I had admired from the early days of my priesthood. As a Capuchin monk in Italy, he had inspired so many people with his strong faith in the Mass and the Eucharist. In the history of the Catholic Church, Padre Pio has been the only priest bearing the stigmata of all five wounds of Christ.

A year before the Midway Chapel was to open, I found myself at a house for priests in Paris, the Foyer Sacerdotal. Come dinner time, we had the choice of forty different places in the dining room. Strangely, one French priest came and sat next to me for the three evenings he spent there.

An American priest, on the third night, asked this French priest for me what kind of work he did. His answer stunned me, "I am Father Andre. I am in charge of promoting the cause of Padre Pio for Sainthood in all of France."

Father Andre went on to tell me, through our American interpreter, that he had known Padre Pio well and had gone regularly for confession to this holy man. From his station wagon, this priest gave me many photos of the stigmatic priest, who had died in 1968. I promised Padre Pio that we would always have his photo in our airport chapel if he brought about its opening. We have kept our promise.

Pope John Paul II beatified Padre Pio in Rome on May 2, 1999. The next step will be canonization of the humble Capuchin monk. We continue to pray to Padre Pio to help us in our Midway Airport Chapel.

In the year 1987 and the first months of 1988, the people of Our Lady of the Snows Parish, located a few blocks from the airport, prayed for the opening of the Midway Chapel. As an associate pastor in the parish, I had shared my dream with them.

At this same time, I visited a parish friend dying of cancer: Bill Sikon. As we sat together, he wrote on a piece of paper, "Chapel—how does it look?"

I said to Bill, "When you get to Heaven in a few days, you will have to pray for us." He died within the week.

A few days later a big breakthrough took place, where before there had not been hope for it. Was Bill working for us in Heaven? His interest in the chapel amazed me. With death at his elbow, Bill was asking about its future.

Mr. Bill Krystiniak, then Alderman of our airport ward,

stepped forward to become a key person in dealing with the Department of Aviation of the City of Chicago. Without him, we would have made little progress in convincing others of the worthiness of a chapel in the airport.

I believe Padre Pio inspired both these Bills to become such devoted friends of the chapel.

Even when Cardinal Bernadin and the city officials gave their permission for religious services to be held in Midway Airport, no one could find a place for the chapel. Was our dream of a place of worship in Midway Airport to stop at this point, after eighteen months of effort and prayer? People in Our Lady of the Snows were offering their pains and sicknesses to God for its opening. We thank all these unknown saints for their unselfish help.

Suddenly, Midway Airlines, under the direction of Mr. David Hinson, came up with a most generous offer. Midway Airlines, to its great credit, gave us the use of one of its gates on Saturday evenings and Sunday mornings. All Midway Airlines employees, and indeed all the airport workers and people of other airlines, have shown the chapel workers a courtesy and a spirit of helpfulness far beyond the call of duty.

We have prayed for the success of the airlines and the good health of their employees and all other airport workers at every Mass offered during these last ten years at Midway.

At the first Mass ever celebrated in Midway Airport—Saturday, July 24, 1988—a young woman guitarist, Miss

Erin Solkowski from Our Lady of the Snows Parish, accompanied the overflowing congregation in song. This was her only visit to the airport chapel. No one else has ever played a musical instrument in the celebration of our Masses.

A few weeks later, Erin's mother told me an amazing story. Erin's middle name is Pio, given at birth. Ann Solkowski needed help at the birth of Erin and prayed to Padre Pio, promising that she would name the child—boy or girl—Pio. Erin was delivered safely. Padre Pio was saying at that first Mass in the airport, "See, I am with you." Thank you, Padre Pio.

In October of 1998 we celebrated the 10th Anniversary Mass and the publication of Volume 1. Over 150 people attended this special event—the largest of any chapel congregation since its founding.

Erin, now married, returned. Once again, the music of her guitar and the sound of her lovely voice praised God, this time in concert with her sister, Fiona, who is also a talented singer. We have had no other musical accompaniment at the chapel in the past ten-and-a-half years. Thank you, Erin and Fiona!

By the end of the year 2000, the Airport Chapel should be in its permanent quarters in the new terminal, presently under construction. Ms. Erin O'Donnell, Deputy Commissioner of Aviation at Midway Airport, has done much to bring the new permanent chapel to actuality.

—Father George McKenna

Midway Airport Acknowledgments

In addition to Padre Pio, Bill Sikon, Bill Krystiniak, the late Joseph Cardinal Bernadin and David Hinson, I would also like to thank and acknowledge others who were instrumental in starting Midway Airport Chapel: Congressman William Lipinski; former Midway Airport Manager, Richard DiPietro; Mayor Richard M. Daley; Richard Guzior; Gene Zell of Zell Printing; Joe Waddell RIP; Reverend Daniel Holihan; Everett G. Rand; Erin O'Donnell; Al Perez; Matt Marich; and the Midway Chapel Volunteer Workers.

Book Acknowledgments

I am indebted to Southwest Airlines which, in coordination with Captain Jack Huffman, Susanne Griffith and Gerry Aumann, transported the first batch of books from Nashville to Chicago free of charge. I appreciate Bill Aumann and his son, Billy, who delivered the twenty boxes to VCA Publishing. Special thanks go to Marie Higgins, who allowed her home to become a makeshift warehouse to store the dozens of cartons from both the first printing and the recent second printing of the first volume.

My sincere appreciation goes to Jeannette Doyle (Adoration Chapel, Queen of Martyrs, Evergreen Park), Donna Dillon (Adoration Chapel, Incarnation, Palos Heights), Vera White (St. Barnabas) and Jeanne Aylward (Our Lady of the Snows) for their ceaseless efforts in promoting Volume One in their respective parishes.

For all my family and friends, too numerous to name, who spread the word—you have my many thanks.

*Father McKenna, James E. Higgins III, and
Erin O'Donnell, Deputy Commissioner, Midway Airport.*

Bring Hope To The World

In the USA, the richest country in the world, many are falling into the sickness of hopelessness. Among young people, suicides—the last stage of despair—continue to increase. Many do not see any reason for living. In buying into the drugs-alcohol-promiscuity culture, they despair of their own self-worth.

Hope is a trust in God for good things to come, such as sufficient health to live in joy and peace, enough money to provide for one's family, enough mental stability to live in harmony with family and other people.

As followers of Christ, we want to bring hope into the world by being people of encouragement. Encouragement means to put a new heart into people for living. Jesus came into the world at a dark point in history and brought His Good News of Hope to all creatures. There is a God Who loves everyone and provides for all His creatures, Jesus would say.

We can give encouragement in a hundred different ways, such as the following true story: On the last day of school at a University, a student was carrying many heavy textbooks across the campus. Suddenly, the books slipped out of his arms and scattered across the sidewalk. At that moment, another collegian, walking by, stopped and picked up the books. With a smile of sympathy, this Good Samaritan carefully put the books back into the arms of the frustrated student. No words passed between them.

Now for the rest of the story! A few years later, these same two men met. The book carrier said to the other man, "Do you remember the day when you helped me with my books? I was on my way to commit suicide, but your kindness and consideration for me convinced me to keep on living."

There is a God Who loves everyone and provides for all His creatures.

Have we not all had that same experience? We weren't on our way to commit suicide, but we felt like throwing in the white towel. Our marriage was sailing on rough seas. Or our long-time, well-paying job was coming to an end. Possibly sickness had weakened our wish to live. Then someone came along to give us a new determination to live by pointing out the possibilities for future good. Maybe they gave us a book or showed us the many hidden talents we had. Possibly they were just kind and listened to our tale of woe.

We all have powers without limit to help others to want to live! Sincere compliments, a show of kindness and respect, helping the new person at work, telling the children and other family members every day, "I love you." Who knows what is going on in the minds of people we meet? Give out many words of praise, only a few words of criticism. Even rude people are crying out for love!

I read these words this past week. They refer to our God of Hope! "Closer is He than breathing, nearer than hands and feet."

Father celebrating Mass at Cenocle Chapel,
fifty yards away from Last Supper Room in Jerusalem.

A Year Of Favor From The Lord

In a recently read Sunday Gospel, Jesus said, "I have come to announce a year of favor from the Lord God." I wish to give two points that will guarantee the reader a year of peace, rejoicing and delight!

In Jerusalem, January 2–11, 1995, I lived at the Center for Biblical Studies, 41 Via Dolorosa (Sorrowful Way). What a thrill to reside on the Way of the Cross! One day, a thought came: I have been living on the Via Dolorosa from my first moment of birth.

At that time (July 12, 1919), I arrived in this world with a physical body open to sicknesses and pain, and with a mind and heart so sensitive to the unloving actions of others. Soon enough, I discovered that original sin made me tend toward evil—with the forces of light battling the powers of darkness within my spirit every day.

Everyone lives on the Via Dolorosa, since we all have the same weakened human nature. Why should we be surprised that sufferings and pain come so often into our lives?

Listen to this first point for a year of favor: Refuse to focus all your thinking on your personal crosses!

When inclined to dwell on these heartaches and physical handicaps, train yourself to turn to other matters in the world about you. Amazingly simple! I have been doing this the last two months and life has blossomed for me with laughter, joy and happiness.

The less time we give to thinking of these crosses, the more energy and consideration we have to pour out on the world about us. As never before, we discover the simple joys of living the first cup of coffee, the excitement of a good book, interest in the lives of other people, a walk in the snow, or a thousand other delights.

I arrived in this world ... with a mind and heart so sensitive to the unloving actions of others.

The second point tells of a rewarding way of living. In Jerusalem, in order to reach my room on the third level, I took an elevator to the second level and then had to climb a steep set of stairs (23 steps) the rest of the way. The angle of the stairs made me think of a ladder leaning against a wall. To avoid a heart attack on these stairs, I would go up three steps, stop to say a Hail Mary, and look at the Jerusalem sky (the stairs were outside the building). At the top I would arrive refreshed after making eight stops.

The second point follows: Take one day at a time! Living the past, future and the day at hand—all at once—won't work. Have confidence! I'm doing it; so can the reader!

Jerusalem old and new, golden Dome of the Rock.

A Surprise Package

We enjoy pleasant surprises! Something unexpected happens and fills empty corners of our hearts with a new delight in living. A few months ago, while cleaning out the back seat of my car, I came upon something in a plastic wrapper. I said, "What's this?" Then, I remembered. My brother had given me this package over a year before. Taking off the wrapping, I found myself holding a statue of Our Lady of the Miraculous Medal about 18 inches tall.

What a happy discovery for me! In recent years I have found much consolation in my devotion to Mary, bestowed with this special title. Now, with this new find, I would have a vision of Our Lady of the Miraculous Medal to set up in my bedroom chapel. Even though a few chips of paint were missing here and there, along with the slight fading of its blue and white colors, the statue had stood the test of time well. In fact, these blemishes gave my statue an air of antiquity!

I hastened at that time some months ago, August 1996, to put my new, precious possession on top of my dresser, a piece of furniture about four feet high. Now, four months later, Our Lady, with her two arms and open hands outstretched at her side, looks down upon me with love and serenity, inviting me to come and share my day's happenings with her. I can put my two elbows on top of the dresser and put my bowed head into my hands in reverence and humility before this vision of Our Lady of the Miraculous Medal. I thus experience much peace!

In Paris, the Cathedral of Notre Dame holds first place in my heart. My second favorite shrine stands in the Rue du Bac. Rue, in French, is street. In this place, the Chapel of Our Lady of the Miraculous Medal attracts crowds of people every day. Nowhere in the world have I witnessed such a spirit of

"Mary, conceived without sin, pray for us who have recourse to thee."

prayer and love for Mary than in the Rue du Bac. Back in 1830, Our Lady appeared to a Sister of Charity, Sister Catherine Laboure, in the sanctuary of this chapel. In these visions Mary had her foot on the head of a snake lying at her feet, no doubt the Devil from the Garden of Eden.

In one visit Our Lady asked Sister Catherine to have a medal made: on the front side, to have the vision of Mary as she came to the nun; on the other side, a symbol of Our Lady's name. These words were to appear on the first side: "Mary, conceived without sin, pray for us who have recourse to thee."

In years gone by, I made this chapel on the Rue du Bac a special place of prayer, asking for help from Mary for my needs, especially those related to my priesthood. So the reader will understand why finding this statue in my car struck me as a message from Our Lady to put new spirit into Her trust in me. She seems to be saying to me, "Be sinless as I, your Mother, am!"

Try God

S ome time ago, May 6, 1994, I reached my Golden Anniversary of 50 years in the Priesthood of the Lord. In these past six months, I found it enlightening to look back over the 53 years to see if I went through certain patterns of action. My discovery might help my readers. Periodically, in years gone by, I fell into dark moods in which my work would appear fruitless, at times almost impossible to carry out. I despaired of being an effective instrument for the Lord.

On looking into these times of negative thinking, I realized that I had been placing the emphasis for success on my personal powers. God with His Might and Glory had been relegated to the sidelines. In these times of darkness, a burst of inspiration would tell me to position God—the Father, the Son and the Holy Spirit—at the center of my operations.

When I did this, a dramatic change would take place in my work. These Three Persons brought grace, light and fruitfulness into my daily work. I didn't see any more success, but a cloud lifted from me. A spirit of joy filled my heart as my whole being delighted in doing God's work as a priest.

Over the years, my trouble lay in the fact that I would forget this truth as time went on. I spent sleepless nights worrying about the work of saving souls. Then the realization would come again that I was trying to accomplish God's work with my own meager resources, forgetting God, the Giver of good gifts. O yes, through all these experiences I always believed in God and His Presence, but, somehow, He was left out of the happenings of the day. I was too wrapped up in my own little world.

Cycles of pessimism and despondency took place through the years, exacting a toll on my spirit of cheerfulness and joy which should be the trademark of any priest. At this late age, probably the most peaceful of my life, I

I spent sleepless nights worrying about the work of saving souls.

know the truth: God will give fulfillment to those conscious of His Willingness to be a Co-worker and help in the ventures at hand.

Does the reader find much despair and gloom in life? Most likely, God (the Father, the Son and the Holy Spirit) with all His Promises of friendship has not been taken at His Word. How does one, no matter what vocation in life, bring God into daily activities? Tell Him every morning, "I can do nothing without Your Help! My abilities and talents come to nothing if You do not stand next to me."

A profound peace, happiness and delight will come into the life of one who does this. Laughter and a spirit of hope claim the heart. Try God! Dio Basta! God is enough!

Chapel of St. James, Paris, France.

My Favorite Shrines In France

In recent times, I carried out a project close to my heart. With two friends—Tom, a layman, and a priest, Father John, both from Albuquerque, New Mexico—I landed in the Paris Orly Airport and rented a car, a Renault. After 20 years of service in the U.S. Infantry, Father John, 48, retired as a lieutenant colonel and entered the priesthood. Tom, 47, is running for Office of District Attorney of Albuquerque, this year of 1996.

The next day, a cold Wednesday, with Tom driving, we headed to the town of Lisieux, 125 miles northwest of Paris, the home of St. Therese, the Little Flower (1873–1897). At Lisieux, we celebrated Mass in the Crypt Church, located under the huge, main Basilica. After prayers to St. Therese in the Basilica (seating capacity 5000) and at her tomb in her convent in the center of town, we went back in the darkness to Paris.

The following day, a Thursday, we headed southeast on the toll road to Ars, still a one-street village made famous by St. John Vianney (1786–1859), the patron saint of all parish priests. After the 300-mile ride, we offered Mass in the very church where the humble

Vianney preached and heard confessions. We prayed for all parish priests of the world.

In late afternoon we drove on to Paray Le Monial, only 35 miles to the northwest, to visit the Shrine of the Sacred Heart and the resting place of St. Margaret Mary (1647–1690). In this quiet, little town, the Lord appeared to Sister Margaret Mary, a Visitation nun, and asked her to spread the message of His wish to be loved and honored.

We arrived in the evening, in time to attend the six o'clock Mass, in the very chapel where the Lord had spoken to Sister Margaret Mary. Our hearts thrilled with the beauty of the Mass, so warmly sung with

... the Lord asked her to spread the message of His wish to be loved and honored.

devotion by the people in the crowded chapel (capacity 200). The next morning, a Friday, we celebrated Mass at the side altar, with the body of Sister Margaret Mary in sight in her glass coffin. I consecrated my priesthood again to the Sacred Heart.

After breakfast, we drove 400 miles southwest to Lourdes, arriving there at 11:00 pm. Early the next morning, a Saturday, and an unseasonably mild day with large numbers of people present, we offered Mass in the Rosary Church, located just over the Grotto of Massabiele, my tenth visit to Lourdes. We prayed much to St. Bernadette Soubirous to strengthen our love for Our Lady.

Reluctantly, we headed for Paris, a ten-hour ride. Our plans called for us to attend the Grand Mass at 10:00 am in Notre Dame Cathedral in Paris on Sunday morning, always a soul-stirring celebration of the Holy Mysteries. In the afternoon, we went to Chartres to pray in the cathedral dedicated to the Mother of God, just a mere 75 miles away to the south of Paris, the largest cathedral in France. I encourage everyone to visit these or other sacred sites for spiritual inspiration and purification.

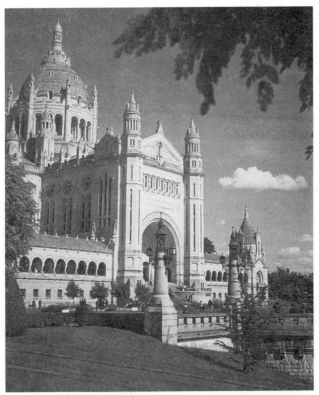

St. Therese Basilica, Lisieux, Normandy, France.

The Rejected One

O ne morning, a short time ago, I stood before a good-sized image of the Sacred Heart in a church sacristy. The glass covering had a crack which ran through the Heart of Christ. How symbolic of the state of the world this is, I thought. As He did many years ago as He looked over Jerusalem, Christ weeps today over the nations of the world for their rejection of Him and His message, possibly over our community as well. He suffers from a broken heart!

In his last years, Francis of Assisi suffered from eye trouble because of his frequent tears. In his crying, he would say often, "Love is not loved!" Would that we felt this poor treatment of Christ in the same way as Francis! Too often the distractions of life dull our minds to this tragedy of life taking place before our eyes. We need to arouse ourselves to the necessity for each one to start a crusade for a recognition of Christ the Sacred Heart.

In September 1994, the Annual Meeting of the International Conference of Airport Chaplains took place in London, England. At its close, I went to Paris with the special intention of visiting Paray La Monial, the place where Our Lord appeared to Sister Margaret Mary in southern France. However, my plans went awry. At noon a fast train, after a two-hour ride, brought me to the city of Macon-Loche, which I thought was close to Paray La Monial but really was 25 miles away.

No bus was scheduled to Paray La Monial for four hours. So, I had to walk around the city for six hours, until I took the 6:00 pm clock train back to Paris. The loneliness I felt on this long day in a strange city reminded me of the loneliness Jesus suffers as He walks through our streets with no one talking to Him.

In his crying, he would say often, "Love is not loved!"

In His appearances at Paray La Monial, Jesus pleaded with Sister Margaret Mary to tell all people how much He wanted their love. In return, He would enrich their lives with gifts and graces beyond description.

Remind all at home that this Lord must rule in the family circle! Set up His Image so all can see and pause before for a prayer of reparation and love. May members of a family kneel before the Sacred Heart for a dedication of themselves to the Lord of Love! I consecrated my priesthood to the Sacred Heart and count this action as my greatest act of wisdom in these past fifty years. I was stationed at St. Margaret Mary Parish for eleven years.

I am going to remind myself frequently of the words of Francis of Assisi— "Love is not loved"—and repeat them through the day. Even a one-person crusade could sweep away the lethargy of taking the Lord, the Sacred Heart, for granted. May we all be a part of this wave of love which would bring light and holiness to all!

A Sacred Memory

As I snuggled down into the warm blankets on a cold Sunday night in January some years ago in the Old City of Jerusalem, I looked forward to the BBC radio program about to begin.

This program, beamed from London to the Middle East through relay stations at this hour, presents a recording of a religious service held someplace in England that Sunday morning.

In a few moments, I hear the pleasant voice of an English priest speaking about Jesus of Nazareth. For some minutes he goes on about the beauty of the Life of the young Preacher from Galilee.

His presentation makes the Friendship of Jesus so appealing. The tone of his voice—its sincerity—strikes a chord in my heart; and to this day, many years later, my heart is still reverberating!

I don't remember the exact words of the priest as the service ends, but in those few minutes something rich and glorious came into my life—perhaps as a blessing for my pilgrimage to the Holy City. His manner of preaching shows that the speaker is drawing from his own experience in living—not from books and notes written by others.

As I doze off to sleep, the English priest's words light up a fire of desire in my heart to continue searching for a deeper relationship with Jesus of Nazareth. More clearly than in many past years, I see that wisdom and true happiness lies in seeking the Face of Christ.

The reader must not think that my life since then has become a neat, little package, all nicely wrapped in satin and linen. I still struggle as much as ever before to persevere in this search for close friendship with the Lord.

The tone of his voice— its sincerity—strikes a chord in my heart ...

Oftentimes I fall back on this sacred memory of a January night years ago in Jerusalem, to give me needed encouragement for the journey. Perhaps the English priest thought his homily had not touched anyone's heart, another wasted effort on his part. Thousands of miles away, his message claimed my heart.

A Glorious Vision Of Life

I will tell a simple story, one that could change our way of living. The July 21st, 1996 Chicago Tribune had an article entitled "Count Your Blessings." The writer told of a young woman recently recovered from a serious illness, quoting her. "When I recovered my health, I embraced life as never before. I smelled the flowers. Every person—everything—was special, wonderful! But then I forgot." The Tribune writer went on to say:

> What happened? The realities of living squelched the glorious vision of life this now healthy woman had for a short time. What were the realities of her life? The kids tracked dirt on the kitchen floor. The rent was due. The car wouldn't start. The boss was bellowing! The dog had fleas. The laundry had to be done.

I cut out this article for my own use and put it into my daily journal. At that time, I was recovering from an illness. Like the woman above, I was smelling the flowers and embracing life as never before. Every person—everything—was special, wonderful. I told myself that I wasn't going to allow the realities of living to take away this glorious vision of life. In days to come, I planned to read and reread this treasured article. These words came often to my lips. "I have tasted the sweetness of that higher way of life. I will not let it go!"

Easier said than done! Now, several months later, my everyday ups and downs are threatening to bring me back to my former, drab way of living. With help from God, I will not let this happen!

... we have powers to learn things and to choose our lifestyles.

Perhaps, without realizing it, our readers have fallen into a trap. We are allowing the realities of life to cheat us out of a glorious vision of life where people and things are special, wonderful. Our way of life has become one of endurance—of just putting in time at home, at work, carrying on a series of dull relationships with others. We are not smelling the flowers!

But, starting today, we can have an outlook in which we see life—each day of living—as a precious gift from God. Count our blessings! We can see, hear, have mobility to get up each morning and move about! In the gifts of our mind and will, we have powers to learn things and to choose our lifestyles. God has made our hearts capable of falling deeply in love with Him and other creatures.

Today, we grow conscious of how realities in our lives can cripple this sparkling vision of living. The laundry has to be done, the heartbreaks of raising a family, the bills to be paid, personal failures, our physical health, problems, misunderstandings with others. Will we cave in under this avalanche of difficult happenings and lose out on a soaring way of life?

Small Miracles Of Amazing Grace

Throughout the year, small miracles of amazing grace take place in our little chapel at Midway Airport with its capacity of 80 people. A sign, at the entrance of our house of worship, could well warn all believers: "Beware, all ye who enter here. Your lives could undergo a sudden change for the better."

Listen to an account of one of these "small miracles of grace." One Sunday morning, January 2, on the Feast of the Three Kings, a young woman in her mid-20s, well-dressed, came up to me as she left the chapel after Mass. She whispered in my ear, "I have been away from the Church for many years, but now I am going to start attending Mass again." With this quick sharing of her heart's secret, she moved on down the Concourse.

Always such a declaration leaves me breathless, as I witness the workings of the Holy Spirit in the heart of a human being. Unaware, perhaps, of what was going to happen, the young woman had seated herself in the chapel and listened to the scriptures and the few words of the priest's homily. In the midst of the worshipers about her, she experienced their faith and peace, as all celebrated the Eucharist together.

For that day, the Gospel told of the thrilling faith journey of the Magi to the feet of the Christ Child. In their homeland of Persia, far away, the Kings, although rich and highly respected, felt an emptiness in their lives. Nothing could satisfy the hunger and thirst within, until they came to the Christ Child, the Prince of Peace.

"I'm just like the Magi," the young woman might have cried out to herself. "I have education, good clothes, friends, excellent health—but still a yearning for something more eats away at my heart. I'm not really happy. As the Magi did, I will go to the feet of the Child of Bethlehem and offer Him the gift of my life."

"Beware, all ye who enter here. Your lives could undergo a sudden change for the better."

I find myself experiencing the same happenings the Magi and the young woman went through. With all the good things of life at my fingertips: food, warm housing, health, enjoyable work, friends and family—at times, I still sense an emptiness in my heart. The Holy Scriptures mention the word *heart* over 700 times. "Why am I anxious, fretful, unhappy?" I say to myself. Then the discovery comes. I have momentarily forgotten the Child of Bethlehem.

On my faith journey, distractions of life have clouded over the Star of Bethlehem. With this realization, I hurry to the feet of the Holy Child and rededicate my life to Him. Peace returns. Dear reader—is this your experience?

Altar of Sorrowful Mother, next to altar of Crucifixion in Holy Sepulcher Church, Jerusalem.

A Story From Jerusalem

Jerusalem, Monday, January 2, 1995. Our group of five arrives in the Holy City after 16 hours of flying time from Chicago by way of St. Louis. An insurance agent, a lawyer, a retired Navyman, a U.S. drug agent on the Mexican border and myself have come on pilgrimage to pray and offer Masses at the holy places.

To our good fortune, we settle in at the Center for Biblical Studies, located at the First Station of the Way of the Cross. I know my fellow travelers well, except for the drug officer who joined us at the invitation of my lawyer friend from Albuquerque, New Mexico. In our eight days in Jerusalem, we experience perfect weather conditions: a bright, warm sun, with temperatures in the high 50s. From our spacious balcony, we see all of the Old City—with the Wailing Wall and the Mosque of Omar just 200 yards away, the Mount of Olives a mile to the east, and the Holy Sepulcher Church three blocks away to the west at the end of the of the Sorrowful Way (Via Dolorosa).

In these wonderful days, we pilgrims share much about our thoughts on life over the three tasty meals

we eat each day at the Center, a place of study oper-
ated by the Sisters of Zion. Underneath our residence
lies the courtyard of Pilate, the actual place where the
Roman Procurator judged Jesus so unjustly. With his
permission, I will relate the story that Bill, the border
patrol officer, told us at dinner one night.

Bill is about 48 years old. Raised a Catholic, he
attended a seminary for one year with hopes of
being an Oblate of Mary Immaculate priest. In 1968,
he served in the military in Vietnam and after that
went on to do police work for the US Government. At
this time, he left behind his
Catholic beliefs and
attended no church ser-
vices. About three years ago,
as Bill and his wife were
driving across the plains of
New Mexico, he saw a little
group of buildings, isolated
on the hillside. Curious, he
drove up the dirt road and discovered a shrine to the
Blessed Mother, built by the local people. Almost
without thinking, he knelt down before Mary's statue
and prayers he had long forgotten came to his lips. At
this time, he had not been to Confession for 23 years.

Suddenly,
he felt something like
an electric shock go
through his body …

Suddenly, he felt something like an electric shock
go through his body, a jarring sensation, much like
one that a fish feels when the fisherman's hook pulls
it up short. From that day on, he took up the practice

of his Catholic faith with a new zest that antagonized his wife, a violent anti-Catholic person. She divorced Bill and left him. Bill's devotion at the Holy Places in Jerusalem inspired us, his fellow pilgrims, and urged us on to prayer. His conversion was not a flash in the pan!

Be careful when kneeling before an image of Mary. Mighty things could happen. A new fire of love could sweep through the heart. Bill's story proved this to me!

Holy Sepulcher church, Christianity's most sacred site.

Emily of Grover's Corners

We are all familiar with the famous theatrical play *Our Town,* by Thornton Wilder. The action takes place in a small town, Grover's Corners, and concerns a young girl, Emily, a life-long resident in the community. Emily dies in giving birth to her child and is buried in the local cemetery.

The Third Act shows Emily sitting on a tombstone, conversing with her mother-in-law, Mother Gibbs. Emily muses, "I would like to go back to town and live again." She talks to the Stage Manager, who permits her to go. Mother Gibbs had tried to dissuade her from going back.

"You will be hurt."

So, Emily returns to Grover's Corners to the day of her twelfth birthday. All things are as they were then.

The table holds many presents for her, but now she is not interested in them. She tries to slow her mother down so that they can share each other for a time, have a chance to communicate. Sadly, mother is busy with many things that occupy her. Emily wants to share the smell of the coffee coming from the kitchen, the tick-tock of the clock, the moments of falling off to sleep and waking, the fragrance and the beauty of the sunflower.

However, these people are so busy living that they don't have any time for these things. In dismay, Emily asks the Stage Manager to take her back up the hill to the cemetery. "O Earth, how wonderful you are! Is there anyone who really lives each minute of the day?"

The Stage Manager answers, "No! Saints and poets, yes, perhaps, to some extent."

This would be the same story of people who would come back and take up their place with us again. They would try to stop us from the hurried, frenzied lives we lead. "Stop," they would say. "You are missing the real joys of living with the kind of life style you have."

"O Earth, how wonderful you are! Is there anyone who really lives each minute of the day?"

Take time out to reassess your life and the direction you are going. Is it necessary to lead a life of quiet desperation? We only have this one life. No more will come our way. Am I really enjoying this style of life I am leading, or not?

Look into the eyes of your loved ones—really look—not just a quick hurried look. Ask what life is dealing up for us. What are we going to make of this gift of life?

Jesus, The Healer Without Equal

Frequently, on Saturday afternoons, a priest friend of mine, a Father Peter Rookey, comes through Midway Airport on his way to St. Louis, where he offers a Healing Mass on Sunday mornings. My friend spends all his time in conducting healing services across our country and the English-speaking world.

Even while traveling, Father Peter wears his cassock, a long brown robe with a hood on the back of it. In his monthly newsletter (International Compassion Ministry, 3121 W. Jackson Blvd., Chicago IL 60612), my friend prints many letters of thanks from people healed in his ministry. This one is from London, England, from a woman healed at a May 24, 1993 meeting:

> Father Rookey, I had been suffering from extreme pain in my head for many years. I could not even comb my hair or touch my head, as it was very painful. I am happy to say that the pain has gone completely, thanks to your prayers.

I am sorry to say that, in all my years as a priest, I have never conducted a public healing service. Call it a lack of faith on my part. Since I have come to know Father Rookey, the thought of healing has taken up my thoughts and made me ask myself, "Why don't you do likewise?"

In the Gospels, Jesus gave first place in His ministry to the work of healing the people in their sicknesses of body and spirit. How richly He rewarded the sick and the demon-possessed with good health when they asked in faith for cures! I conducted my first public healing service ever in our Airport Chapel by asking the congregation to hold up loved ones in need of healing. With a brief prayer, and a protest of our complete faith in Him, I begged the Lord to heal these sick of body and spirit.

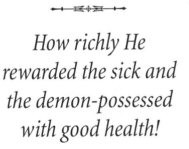

How richly He rewarded the sick and the demon-possessed with good health!

This prayer of healing will have a frequent place in our Airport Chapel Liturgy in the days to come. Father Rookey has convinced me that the Lord of the Gospels wants His ministry of healing to go on for the sake of people broken by illnesses. Every person, young and old, can be a healer.

"Lord, my little girl is sick at home, please cure her." "My son is possessed with demons. He cannot sleep at night. Please touch him and make him whole again." Say these requests with total faith in the Loving Master of the Gospel stories. He will respond to this overwhelming show of faith by using His Powers for healing.

As I finished my morning Mass at the airport this past Sunday, along came Father Rookey on his way home from healing services in Georgia.

The Story Of
The Lemon Cream Pie

We remember loving people and their loving deeds. Back in the 1930s in the middle of the Great Depression, my Aunt Marie (also my godmother) would always bring a big lemon cream pie on her visits to our home. I had a special taste for the luxury dessert. Aunt Marie knew! All this took place some sixty years ago; but every time I eat lemon cream pie, I think of my loving Aunt Marie and bless her. Pretend that we could come back in a second life, be reincarnated, with all the wisdom and experience of the first life in our possession. If God would ask me at this time, "What gift would you like to have? Ask for anything you wish!"—I wouldn't ask for riches, high social position, a sharp intelligence. My request would be: "Lord, make me a loving person!"

Why this gift? The people who helped me the most in life were loving persons, such as my Aunt Marie, teachers who spoke positive, encouraging words and respected me despite my failures. In the presence of gentle friends, I found myself at ease. Only the love of my parents and family made it possible for me to grow and mature in a normal way.

We need not come back in a second life to bring the gift of love into our lives. In this present day, all of us can freely choose to be loving persons. Take out "loving" and put in any of these words: patient, forgiving, friendly, encouraging, rejoicing, unselfish.

Loving persons accomplish the most good in life. They bring peace to themselves, because they refuse to compete with others by trying to have the upper hand in all happenings of life. In boosting others, they share in their accomplishments and bring extra joy into their lives.

I wouldn't ask for riches, high social position, a sharp intelligence.

I remember a little girl receiving the Eucharist in her hand. In the middle of her palm, she had written the word "love." She will have a lasting place in my memory. Look back in life and notice the power of loving actions for good.

As we rise from bed in the morning, a good prayer would be: "Lord, I want to be a loving person today, with only loving thoughts in my mind and loving words on my lips." Have confidence that we can act out this ideal.

A Blockbuster Of A Resolution

The beginning of the New Year ushers in the time for making resolutions with the hope of bettering our lives. "I'm going to diet." "Less TV." "No smoking." "Some exercise every day." Promises like these only touch the outer edges of life, the periphery of our life experience. Consider something more life changing! I want to propose a resolution that will go directly to the heart of life, to the core of our being. The one I offer sounds deceptively simple and goes like this, "I wish to be a loving person." When I took this resolution and tried to live it out each day in years past, I brought the peace and happiness of Heaven into my heart.

A few nights ago, on a Christmas program, Dione Warwick sang a song, "What The World Needs Now Is Love." This heart-tugging melody reminds us that we do have a cure for all the violence about us in the world today. That cure is love and respect for each other. No matter what our age, schooling, or social position, we all have the ability to be loving persons.

In the past, after taking this resolution, I found myself waking in the morning, with feelings of excitement about all the opportunities I would have that day to be a loving person. Kindness, gentleness and forgiveness would be the key words in my mind for the hours ahead.

All of a sudden, my thoughts, words, and actions came under closer scrutiny, with the conviction that anger, hatreds, and ill will could have no place in my life. Because of my resolution, I found it easy to put these out of my mind.

As I tried to show respect and consideration for others and their feelings, I came to appreciate more my own person and my own gifts. If the reader takes this resolution to heart, a light and beauty will shine forth from the face that will attract new friends and bring a delight to life.

> *"I wish to be a loving person."*

One may wonder whether all this will happen from the taking of such a simple resolution as the one offered, "I wish to be a loving person." Yes, all this and much more.

"Did I fill the world with love?"

At death, we will have much consolation if we will be able to say, "Yes, I did the best I could."

Good health comes to those who make such a resolution. We stop trying to outachieve everyone about us. We drop a spirit of competitiveness that brings stress to the inner workings of our bodies. On the contrary, we rejoice when others do well and urge them on with sincere words of praise and encouragement.

Rock of betrayal, Church of All Nations, Gethsemane

Choosing A Hero Is Most Worthwhile

This past week, Tiger Woods, the new sensation in the world of golf, came to our town and won the Western Open Golf Title—to the delirious joy of his countless fans. Only 21 years of age, Tiger has captured the hearts of thousands with his self-disciplined commitment to a life-long dream of excellence in golf. Through the four days of the Tournament, people of all ages lined the fairways, cheering on their new-found hero, a smiling, poised young man. Children have begun asking for golf clubs! Choosing someone to be our hero, especially one of high ideals, can bring many good changes into our life. In the above Tournament, those thousands of fans forgot their own interests and fears to cheer for the success of another human being. In their wildest dreams, these enthusiastic followers began to plan for success in their own lives.

I encourage everyone to take Jesus of Nazareth as a Hero to follow and imitate. What a fantastic Person Jesus is, One to cheer for, the Lord of Lords, the King of Kings, the Master of the Universe! In a recent weekend Gospel, His neighbors in His own village of

Nazareth reject Jesus and try to kill Him. "A Prophet is not received in His own town," Jesus cries out. In our heart of hearts, we are all seeking a hero we can look up to and enthuse about. Why not choose this exciting person, Jesus, Whose gifts and talents we can never exhaust!

Unfortunately, many picture this process of picking Christ as a Hero a tedious, dull operation. Not so! In Scripture, Mary Magdalen called Jesus at the Resurrection Time: "Rabboni"(Beloved Teacher). We begin our following of the Lord by actually developing an affectionate relationship with Him as Mary Magdalen did. "Lord, I love You with my whole heart and soul." We can say this every day in season and out of season!

In our heart of hearts, we are all seeking a hero we can look up to and enthuse about.

When I begin to think of Christ as a too serious Person to get close to, I look at a holy card a friend gave me, entitled, "The Smiling Christ." From the card, Jesus looks out at me with a heart-warming smile, so much as to say, "No need to be afraid of Me. I want you for a close friend." I smile back and cry out with enthusiasm, "Thanks, Lord, I want to follow You always and push Your Cause in the world about me." Incredible things happen!

With Jesus as our Hero, we attend Mass on week-ends, not because we have to, but rather to give witness to our belief in His Presence among us. I share my daily life with the Master, "Lord, how will I deal with this difficult situation facing me today? Show me what You would do!" So few people take the Gentle Christ as their Hero! What a tragedy to miss out on this way of living!

Ecce Homo–Behold The Man

A few days ago, I visited a Franciscan Monastery in Libertyville, Illinois, where there is continuous adoration of an exposed Blessed Sacrament in the church. In a side chapel an exquisite mosaic, an art work made up of small colored pieces of stone, pictures Christ after His beating by the Roman soldiers. Life size, the Lord stands on the wall with a purple cloak, a crown of thorns, His hands tied in front of Him, a look of anguish on His Face. Pilate showed the innocent Christ to the crowds with the words, "Behold the Man." What a heartbreaking sight this mosaic was, even to me, in that quiet chapel, 2000 years later.

Many times in the Gospels the Lord cried out, "The Kingdom of God is at hand." For me the best definition of the Kingdom of God came from a radio broadcast I was listening to while driving along the highway some years ago. "Wherever Jesus and His Name are loved and honored, there is the Kingdom of God." So, even today, if we make Christ the center of our lives, respect and love Him, we have His Holy Kingdom in our hearts, our homes and in our communities. We need not wait for Heaven to enjoy the

Kingdom!

Many writers say that we live in a post-Christian age. In other words, Christ is a "has been." The Pilates of the 1990s hold Him up before jeering crowds. "*Ecce Homo,* behold the Man!" People deny His Kingship, that He deserves our service and love! We can meet this challenge of indifference to Christ by daily pledging Him our undying love and by living our lives according to His ways of holiness.

In countries around the world—Iran, China, Cuba, Burma, just to mention a few—Christians are going to prison, and sometimes dying, for their giving witness of love for Christ the King. This is a wake-up call for holiness of life for all of us who profess to be

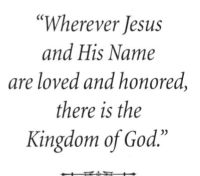

"Wherever Jesus and His Name are loved and honored, there is the Kingdom of God."

citizens of the Kingdom of Christ. "Lord, help us to walk in Your ways of holiness." If renewal is necessary, be aware of the mighty possibilities for change in our lives. Within us lie the seeds of greatness, if only we make Christ the shining Lord and King of our days.

A seagoing ship must go into dry-dock periodically to have the barnacles (sea creatures) scraped from its sides. If this is not done, these creatures will slow up the progress of the ship considerably. As human beings, if we are to be Proclaimers of the Kingship of

Christ, we need to scrape off attitudes of thinking and patterns of acting that hold us back from announcing to all that Christ is alive.

Let us pray: "I will kneel before an Image of Christ the King and offer my complete dedication to Him. I will keep the Commandments, the moral laws. These will be my guidelines as I live out my life in The Kingdom!"

Mount of Olives and Garden of Gethsemane,
across from the old city.

A Bishop Leaves Me With An Inspiring Thought

In early June, 1994, I joined with 550 other Chicago priests for a four-day series "Convocation Days" at Pheasant Run in nearby St. Charles, Illinois. Part business and part social, the "Days" provide us priests with a chance to spend time together, celebrate a joyful Mass each day and listen to some speakers. I thoroughly enjoyed this relaxing experience which Cardinal Bernardin hopes to continue every two years!

Of all the words I heard from the homilies and lectures, I most remember one line, spoken by Bishop Untener of Saginaw, Michigan. This talented man, still a hockey player at the age of fifty and with one foot missing, spoke these words one morning. "Do not allow your prayers to dead end in Jesus." I had never heard this idea put into these words!

Yes, certainly continue prayers every day to Lord Jesus; but, also, go beyond Jesus to God, the Father, and God, the Holy Spirit. The Bishop was saying that the full picture of the Kingdom includes not only

Jesus, but also the Father and the Spirit. Since that day the Bishop spoke, I have, as never before, been more conscious of all Three Persons in my daily prayers, with a resultant increase of appreciation and love for Them. A new excitement and enthusiasm has entered into my pursuit of God and His Love!

This past Thursday, I found myself out on a golf course in the middle of a heavy rainstorm, standing with others in a shelter. God, the Creator, provided me with an exciting meditation on His Greatness and Genius. In the sky above, threatening, dark clouds paraded their beauty, accompanied by booming music of thunder and the dagger-like thrusts of lightning. In the cascading rain, I could smell its sweetness, as it washed clean the countryside. "What a Great Person the Father is!" I cried out to myself. All these spectacular happenings of Nature reflect in a small, infinitesimal way His Creative and Loving Mind. I want to know This Person better!

Consider the marvelous truth that the Holy Spirit lives within each one.

Yes, the words of Bishop Untener were working in me. "Don't allow your prayers to dead end in Jesus." Consider the marvelous truth that the Holy Spirit lives within each one. Wherever we see love in the world, we know the Spirit is close at hand. Every weekend, in Midway Airport, I notice blind travelers with their "seeing-eye" dogs. How devoted and concerned for the safety of their owners these wonderfully trained animals are as they guide their sightless masters to their planes.

The Holy Spirit has infused into their hearts the power to serve their blind masters until death. Each day, I am more conscious of begging the Spirit to work miracles of love in my poor, human heart. Thanks, Bishop Untener!

The Ever-Present Cross In Our Lives

January, 1995, in my visit to the Holy City of Jerusalem, I stayed with the Sisters of Sion at this address, 42 Via Dolorosa (Sorrowful Way). Yes, I would walk out of the front door of my residence (Center of Biblical Study), go down two steps and find myself immediately at the First Station of the Way of the Cross, where the bruised and beaten Jesus walked years ago.

Oftentimes in my stay there last January, I hiked along this narrow, winding, always ascending, rocky road, imagining myself with a heavy cross on my shoulders. I wanted to get in practice for my own personal Way of the Cross back in Chicago or wherever, a journey that was bound to come to me.

In a past Bulletin, I noted that we all live on our own, personal Via Dolorosa (the Sorrowful Way). Life deals out crosses of all kinds to peoples of all ages and in all positions of authority. Think of Cardinal Bernardin! On a wall, just outside my residence on the Sorrowful Way, a plaque read: "Jesus is searching for someone who will humble himself as He did and lovingly bear his cross. Will you be His disciple?"—in four languages.

Recently, in the last two months, I have come upon my own personal physical cross—not life threatening, so please, no sympathy. Something unforeseen! I won't share it with you at this time. My practice walks on the Way of the Cross last January have helped me greatly in bearing with this undesired happening. I have asked the Holy Spirit to explain how I can deal with this new chapter in my life in a positive way.

Some weeks ago, we saw Cardinal Bernardin on TV newscasts, moving along the Way of the Cross on his first visit to the Holy Land. Now he has entered his own Via Dolorosa. In these days of confinement and prayer, his thoughts must turn often to this time he spent in Jerusalem, especially on the Sorrowful Way.

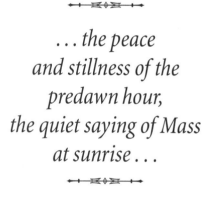

... the peace and stillness of the predawn hour, the quiet saying of Mass at sunrise ...

Again, I am speaking about myself, personally. What am I learning from my own recently arrived cross? I pray more. This time in prayer will provide the spiritual strength I need to do well by my cross. I remember the words on the plaque: "Jesus is looking for someone who will willingly bear his cross. Will you be his disciple?"

Another bonus I have experienced sounds like this: I am living one day at a time as I have never lived out this philosophy before. "Dear God, just get me through this day!" One day doesn't present a lot of hurdles!

As never before, I taste the little joys of living: a cup of coffee slowly sipped, the peace and stillness of the predawn hour, the quiet saying of Mass at sunrise, a book of stimulating thoughts, a certainty of help from the Holy Spirit.

"Unless you take up your cross and follow Me, you cannot be my disciple!"

Religion, A Personal Commitment To Christ

When I was a boy of eight or nine years of age, I envied the children on the block with no religion. These boys and girls had an ideal life style—with no church to attend on Sundays, no Ten Commandments to follow, and no necessity of going to a priest to tell their sins. I had to go to church, try to keep the Commandments, and then tell my sins to the priest! Often the thought came: Why did I have to be born into a family with faith?

Then the Holy Cross nuns taught us children how Jesus of Nazareth stands behind the Ten Commandments with these words on His lips, "If you love Me, keep the Commandments." Suddenly, I saw this long list of "do's" and "don'ts" not as an enumeration of restrictions, but as a loving posting of directions to happiness and peace. I realized that by following these wishes of Christ, I could deepen my friendship for Him.

The way of life that the boys and girls with no religion followed oftentimes led to selfishness, self-gratification and, sometimes, self-destruction. As the years went on, life ceased to have meaning for many of my friends on the block.

About 40 years ago, I read a pamphlet entitled "Are We Really Teaching Religion?", written by a Frank Sheed, an outstanding Catholic layman of that time. This little essay has never left my possession, because I treasured the theme of the article. I read it just a few days ago. The main thrust of the essay came to this: "Children are leaving religion classes with a great amount of information about faith in God, but, too often they have not developed a warm Friendship for Jesus of Nazareth."

Why not such a loving relationship with the Christ of the Gospels?

After leaving eighth grade or High School, Mr. Sheed wrote, the young people drop all this intellectual data as so much baggage and stop attending worship services. If Jesus of Nazareth had become a close, loving Friend, the youth would feel a sudden distress in their hearts for His disappearance from their lives. Religion can't simply be dry bones information, but, rather, a loving, personal commitment to a Person, Jesus of Nazareth.

Young people are capable of strong, loyal friendships. How easily they spend an hour on the telephone, conversing with schoolmates! They can do this because of their interest in the lives of other young-sters. Why not such a loving relationship with the Christ of the Gospels?

Let the religion teachers of your children or grand-children know about this book. Buy extra copies and give them to the parents of children in your acquain-tance. If the young people love Christ dearly, it will be sufficient.

Called To Be Healers

One day, in the Paris Subway, the Metro, I witnessed a perfect example of a healing. At the height of the rush hour, a woman in front of me lost all her oranges from a broken bag. "*Voila* (Oh just see)," she cried in dismay as she saw the fruit rolling in every direction among the feet of the commuters. Wonder to behold, in their rush, people stopped to pick up the oranges and brought them back to the distraught woman. At the sight of all the fruit once again in her arms, she burst out with cries of joy, "*Merci, merci!* (Thanks, thanks!)." A true healing had taken place. All the parts came back to form a wholeness. A splintered heart was renewed!

Little did the kind commuters realize the healing they had brought about by their simple actions. I picked up one of the oranges. Be aware of the powers we have to give peace and comfort to our suffering sisters and brothers. In the Gospels, every page tells of a healing action of the Young Preacher from Nazareth.

I used to envy the medical people for their ability to effect healing in their sick patients. As time went on, I saw myself as a healer, equipped to bring a wonderful wholeness into the lives of people I meet every day. A cheerful word to a depressed person can chase the darkness from his mind. For one grieving for a deceased loved one, I can offer a hug and an expression of sympathy. My ever-present spirit of forgiveness gives other human beings new hope for the future, as in their weaknesses they cause me pain. In the words above, I speak for everyone.

In our efforts to be healers, we imitate the Master, Jesus of Nazareth, the Divine Healer. What comfort a parent gives to a sobbing child hurt by the cruelties of schoolmates with a hug and a kiss! The expression "I love you" works small miracles in hearts troubled by low self-esteem. Even such a small happening as a smile from someone serving me food, a waitress or a flight attendant raised my low spirits and made me want to go on living.

A well-timed letter, a loving phone call, a short visit to a sick bed . . .

Each day, set out on the journey of healing as the Master did in His time on earth. Be interested in all peoples coming across our path as Jesus was! A well-timed letter, a loving phone call, a short visit to a sick bed—all these can effect a marvelous healing in the lives of people about us. Nothing will give our own hearts so much peace and consolation as our efforts to be healers!

A friend says, "I'm sick." Take the hands of that person.

"We will pray now!"

Sacre Coeur, Paris, France.

The Best Of All Blessings

I have celebrated Mass many times in the little church of Bethany, a small community, just three miles east of Jerusalem. The Bethany story tells of the friendship of Lazarus and his sisters, Martha and Mary, with the young Rabbi, Jesus of Nazareth. This family welcomed Him to their home for nourishment and rest. Jesus accepted their invitations and came there often, after preaching in the Holy City for long hours. I treasure this part of the Gospels.

From the Bethany story, I learn that the Lord wanted friends and human relationships. In his days on earth, the human part of Him desired and needed companionship and conversations. Jesus, the God-man, still wishes for warm friendships with His followers, you and me. If we open the doors of our hearts and homes to Him, He comes to eat and drink with us. He has many ideas He sorely wishes to share with us.

In our Bethany hearts and homes, He finds consolation as He sees the love of the family members for each other. He notices the holy images there, especially of His Blessed Mother, the kind of books and

TV programs the family indulges in. This same Jesus Who visited the Lazarus family puts all at ease with His kindness and gentleness.

Are we talking about a land of make-believe? No, we speak about the 1990s in Midwest USA! I see friendship with the Lord as the best of all blessings. Friends ask why I go back to Jerusalem so often. My answer sounds like this: "I want to strengthen my closeness with the God-man, Jesus of Nazareth. No one who ever lived can approach His wonderful qualities of mind and heart. His friendship brings peace to me!"

Friendship means a two-way action. We must strive to make this relationship with Christ come alive, by daily

All this can take place in a glorious atmosphere of joy and lightheartedness.

conversing with Him in a person-to-Person way, and by doing our best to follow His ways of holiness shown to us in the Ten Commandments. All this can take place in a glorious atmosphere of joy and lightheartedness. Associate happiness with Christ!

How sad to see so many missing out on the Bethany story! Christ, for them, has become a museum piece, a tale from antiquity with no meaning for the present age. Taken in by the swirl of modern life, its distractions and peer pressure, many, or most, of our young people avoid the challenge of bringing Christ into their lives. If I, the writer, were a young man again, I would probably be doing the same. Do they think that if they accept Jesus as a warm Friend, this might shake up their consciences and rob them of complete freedom of action? Jesus gives true freedom!

For all, Christ stands before us, with Hands outstretched to us in friendship!

Indifference of the World Toward Christ

In the splendid D'Orsai Museum in Paris, France, one of the top-ten-ranked museums in the world, hangs an unusual painting of Christ. In a rectangular frame, the painting measures seven feet in length and two feet high and rests on the wall at eye level. The Lord lies stretched out on a table, all washed and clean, about to be placed in His tomb. What a striking piece of work! As I stood only a foot away from the masterpiece, I could clearly see the muscles and the bluish veins in the legs and arms, along with the perfection of the artist's work in His Face and other parts of His Body. How truly human Jesus was!

In my visits, I always stood off to the side and wondered how many people would stop and admire this Image of the Lord. Never did anyone come, at least in my time. People were rushing by in search of beauty and inspiration, and were passing by the Source of all Happiness. I thought this experience made up a good parable of life. In our modern day world, peoples of all ages have grown indifferent to Christ, the Lord of

Lords and the King of the Universe. We can all fall prey to this blindness of heart!

From my own life, I can give you an illustration of this blindness. Several months ago, friends gave me a gift of a wristwatch, an unusual one because the face of the watch showed an appealing Image of the Lord looking out at me with His arms outstretched. For some weeks I was enthralled with my new possession, frequently through the day gazing at this Holy Image and enjoying the consolation of His Presence. Suddenly, this past month, the sad realization came to me that I was taking the Face of Christ for granted. Yes, I looked at the watch for a time, but passed over the Person on its face. These days, I am putting fresh fuel on my fire of love toward this Friend!

After a while, only a shell of the once delightful relationship remains.

In past years, the news of Weeping Virgins, even here in Chicago, has caught our attention. If true, Mary weeps because people have forgotten the love and devotion due to Her Son. Does she weep over my way or your way of indifference toward the Messiah, Her Child of Bethlehem?

Marriage experts all agree on a deadly disease that threatens every married couple, a terrible malaise of spirit in which one or both spouses start taking each other for granted. The little marks of respect and consideration which keep love alive and flourishing disappear from married life. After a while, only a shell of the once delightful relationship remains. Breakup ahead! Our relationship with Jesus of Nazareth follows the same rules. Unless we offer daily our love, our hopes, our sacrifices to stay holy, to Christ, we can lose that closeness we once enjoyed.

Holy Spirit, Open My Mind To Possibilities Around Me

In speaking of physical health, all medical doctors agree on one point: exercise is a must. "Use your heart or lose it." Since retiring eight years ago, I have rented a condominium in a three-story complex at 99th South Pulaski Road. I was totally convinced of my need for exercise, but weather conditions kept me far from my ideal—too rainy, too cold, too hot, too snowy, too inconvenient to go down three floors to street level.

Just recently, the thought came to me out of the blue: what about the corridor just outside my door. It is long enough, about 50 yards, half a football field, heavily air-conditioned in hot weather, warm in winter. So I began my daily walks for 30 minutes at a time. My level of good health jumped up immediately. I was actually thrilled at this discovery of how to get my walking in. All this at my own front door! Oh, if I had only done this starting eight years ago, how strong I would be today! Just plain dumbness on my part!

In regard to the health of our soul, spiritual writers tell of the absolute necessity of making Jesus, the

Great Prophet from Nazareth, the center of our life. On the stage of life, we are to focus the spotlight of our love and attention on this Gentle Person of the Gospels. All other persons stand in the dark, in the background. Here we see the Savior offering us His Love and Friendship. We need but say "yes" and He will come, capture our hearts and draw us under His spell of goodness and righteousness. We follow up this "yes" with a daily sharing of the happenings of our life with Jesus.

How much happier I would be today if I had done so!

In this brief message, we read how we can make glorious our interior life by accepting the Lord's invitation to be a loving friend. In the opening part above, I recounted how I allowed the circumstances of life to keep me from daily exercise, so needed for physical health. If I had only thought clearly, I could have seen how simple it was to find a place for exercise.

We can easily allow the conditions of life to make us deaf and blind to this chance of a lifetime, like: too much work to do, too little time, too many responsibilities, or that old favorite, "I'm not the praying type." This invitation is open to all peoples of all ages. We might not hear these words again for another eight years and then recall sadly, "O yes, I remember reading these words in the Midway Airport Chapel

Bulletin. I was too busy living to take the words to heart. How much happier I would be today if I had done so."

Thrill at the simplicity of carrying out the above resolution! Jesus stands before us. "Why are you making Me an alabaster statue, a thing with no hearing, no sight, and no understanding, something of antiquity. I am fully alive, alert to all the goings on of your life. Only share your life with Me." Remember how I began this essay, my sadness at missing out on exercise available at my front door.

Totally Yours, O God

O ur present Holy Father, John Paul II, has these two Latin words—Totus Tuus (Totally Yours)—on his coat of arms. As a young man, preparing for the priesthood in an underground seminary in war-torn Poland, he knelt before Christ in the great Cathedral in Krakow and consecrated himself to the Lord of the Gospels. Since then, he has not looked backward or watered down any of his original commitment to the Master.

On the mornings of my receiving the three Major Orders—the Subdeaconate, the Deaconate, and the Priesthood—I rose early and went to the Main Chapel in the center of the Seminary Campus at Mundelein, Illinois. A space of five months elapsed between the reception of each of these Orders. Each time, I meditated on the appearance of the Risen Lord to His Apostles at the seashore in Galilee. At this visit, Jesus called Peter aside and asked the kneeling Apostle, three times, "Peter, do you love Me?" Peter had denied his Lord three times. The Gentle Christ used this way of questioning to bring peace to Peter's heart. "Yes, Lord, You know I love You," said Peter, each time.

On these three historic mornings, I pictured myself kneeling before the Lord, with Him asking me the same question three times, "George, do you love Me?" I placed my hands into His Hands and said, "Yes, Lord, I do love You." Down through these last fifty-one years in the priesthood, I found the memory of these meditations immensely helpful and consoling. I say to myself, I started out with a "Totus Tuus" (completely Yours) attitude in the priesthood; with God's help, I will finish in the same way.

Only God knows how well or how poorly I have kept this initial consecration up to present time! In His Public Life, Jesus said to a number of people, "Come, follow Me." Many gave excuses for not following immediately: "Lord, let me bury my father!" "Allow me to go home and say good-bye to my family!" Jesus was not happy with these responses, "No one putting his hand to the plow and looking backwards is fit to be My disciple."

... with no other desire in your heart than to serve Him faithfully until death.

Our teachers in the Seminary told us seminarians that a total commitment to God makes the work of serving Him much easier. In times of temptations of all sorts, we will answer quickly, without hesitation, "I will serve only the Lord, my God." If I am only half-committed, I could dilly-dally with my response and end up compromising my ideals.

Each day, kneel in spirit or actuality before the Lord and tell Him that you are a "Totus Tuus" disciple of His, with no other desire in your heart than to serve Him faithfully until death. The attractions of the world lose their strong appeal in the face of such dedication to God. An immense joy will fill your heart!

The Holy Spirit
A Messenger From God

On Friday, May 26, 1995, a woman in our apartment complex died suddenly at the age of 84. On the way to the hospital, Mary—May she rest in peace—reminded her daughter, "Be sure to give my painting to Father McKenna." A few days ago, Mary's son-in-law brought her precious painting, her treasure for 34 years, to my door. Quite sizable, it measures 4 feet by 2 feet.

The artist shows a close-up view of Christ standing at the door of a house in the woods at night time, with the moon shining through the trees. The Lord is about to knock on the door. Ten minutes after I received this piece of art, I sat down to write something about this unusual happening. As Pentecost was approaching, I had been praying to the Holy Spirit to inspire me with a deeper love for God. Maybe this gift had a message from the Spirit for me.

As I began to write, I caught sight of a few words of attractive printed type on a paper underneath a jumble of twenty other papers and cards on the table next to me. For some reason, I pulled out this sheet, risking an avalanche of papers to the floor. The headlines on the narrow strip of paper read, "Surrender Prayer," with these words in the first lines: "Come to Me, My friend! I call you to a deeper surrender of yourself. I call you to come to Me."

The thought came to me that Christ is knocking on the door of my heart and asking for a total surrender of my life to Him. My surrender, in days past, had been incomplete. "Yes, Lord, I give my life to you, but make sure that I keep all my senses, sight, mind, speech, hearing and mobility. I want a painless death." These past days, I am offering myself completely to Christ without putting in some fine print conditions. Take everything, Lord!

> *"Spirit of Love, help me to be alert to your work in my life."*

Believe that, in the daily happenings of life, the Holy Spirit has precious messages for us. Keep eyes open and door to heart ajar. Look out on life with eyes filled with anticipation of many life changing experiences happening to us. Much faith is needed!

How will this happen? A few examples: Someone loans us a book on God. We recover from a sickness with a sense of gratitude. A close skirmish with death leaves us breathless. In traveling, we see new ways of doing things. One close to us begins a renewal of life.

A valued friend dies.

If we leave the Holy Spirit out of our thinking, we can miss out on terrific learning experiences. "Spirit of Love, help me to be alert to your work in my life."

Jesus Of Nazareth Is Passing By

In the spacious dining room of the Major Seminary of the Chicago Archdiocese at Mundelein, Illinois, a huge oil painting covers the entire west wall. This work of art shows much blue sky and a roadway. At the curbside, some people are standing, others sitting—all looking at someone or some thing not shown in the painting. A long shadow falls across the road.

As a seminarian, I didn't understand the masterpiece for a long time, not being curious enough to ask about it. Too many other new experiences, as a first-year man in the seminary, were occupying my thoughts. Finally, one day, I walked up to the painting and discovered the title on the bottom corner of the work: "Jesus Of Nazareth Is Passing By."

By the time I left the seminary as a priest in 1944, this painting had burned itself and its message into my mind—never to be forgotten, always to be treasured, a life-long influence for good in my life ahead. Especially in times of darkness and confusion, this mighty work of some artist would flash through my thoughts and remind me that Jesus of Nazareth is passing by. Yes! He is present in the Tabernacle, in the Eucharist, in the Words of Scripture.

During a three-month Pastoral Ministry Course in Dublin, Ireland, in 1975, I met a Father Michael Hollings, a priest-lecturer from London, England. He impressed me the most of all the thirty-two speakers I listened to. His constant theme came across like this: Spend time with the Lord before the Tabernacle; He is passing by with His healing graces, gifts of encouragement, peace and love, —the same Gentle Person of the Gospels. Again and again, as I heard his words, the painting from the seminary dining room occupied my thoughts.

The dark side of daily living gave me the chance to turn to the Lord passing by . . .

Some may say, "Father, you often write of trying times in your priesthood— misunderstandings, unhappy work situations and other challenges in your work in the Church." That is correct! As I look back over 50 years, I am glad that I never had perfect control over the happenings in my life. The dark side of daily living gave me the chance to turn to the Lord passing by and beg Him for help in a hundred different ways.

The reader, too, has to deal with the rough side of life. No one has perfect conditions for living, with the weaknesses of original sin in everyone about us. Turn to the Christ of the Gospels. We can reach out to Him in prayer from any place we find ourselves.

What Price Can We Put On Kindness?

O n Friday, March 28, 1998, a hundred priests gathered for the Funeral Mass of a fellow priest, Father Joe Ryan, 80, in St. Walter's Church on Chicago's South Side. The overflow crowd of friends attested to the fact that Father Joe had been a much loved priest.

As I sat there in church that cold, windy morning, my thoughts went back 65 years to my first year in Quigley Seminary, located then close to Holy Name Cathedral. On that October afternoon, in the year 1933, a long line of us boys was waiting to shoot a basketball in our pint-sized gym.

Suddenly, a bigger boy came along and pushed me out of line. Rude. At that moment, a second-year boy showed up and put me back in place. Little did I know that this incident would forever remain in my memory. The kindness of the older boy, Joe Ryan, has haunted my mind all through the ensuing years.

There is something Christ-like about kindness, doing a favor for someone, maybe even a stranger. I was a little nobody back in 1933, a stranger to Joe

Ryan, but he took time to help me. That's why we wish to know Jesus of Nazareth as well as we can. We want to be a person like Him, ready to show consideration to other human beings. On every person's back, we can put the word "fragile"! We are so easily hurt and crushed by the happenings of life!

One day, the Pharisees brought a woman taken in adultery to Jesus. "Such a woman should be stoned," they told the Master. Stooping down, the Lord began to write their sins in the sand. Soon, only Jesus and the woman stood alone. With gentle voice and compassion, He told her, "I do not con-demn you, but sin no more." I sure like the soothing way Jesus treated her tortured spirit. If He had agreed to her stoning, I would have been brokenhearted. Instead, He protected her from the vultures seeking her blood. I feel like shouting, "Glory! Alleluia!" How wonderfully kind is Our Savior!

"There is only one Commandment. You've got to be kind."

Kindness, the full flowering of all the human vir-tues, makes a person so attractive, so appealing, so winning! I wanted to get up at Father Joe Ryan's Funeral Mass and tell of my meeting him 65 years ago in a crowded gym. Tears came easily during this Mass of the Resurrection. Kurt Vonnegut, the noted writer, put it well: "There is only one Commandment. You've got to be kind."

Just in front of me at this Mass sat Father John Hayes, 92, my all-time hero. Back in 1933, I said to myself as I saw this priest in the Quigley Chapel, "That's the kind of priest I would like to be—quiet, prayerful, respectful of students, kind." I didn't even know his name. I was 100% correct in choosing him for my ideal of a kind person.

Demons Are Close By

I n the past two weeks, a jury of twelve judged Timothy McVeigh guilty of the murder of some 160 people, including 19 children. A fuller picture tells of the maiming of hundreds of others and of the sorrow brought to thousands of family members. Picture this man as a young boy in the innocence of childhood! What took possession of his heart in the time he was growing to manhood?

How could this sadistic evil enter his heart? We encounter here the mystery of evil. Certainly Timothy McVeigh allowed his heart to fall into darkness and become the playground of Satan and the evil spirits. As we read this horror story, we should say to ourselves, "There, but for the grace of God, go I." Yes, we human beings, made in the Image of God, can fall into the deepest pits of depravity if we allow the demons control of our lives.

For years, I played golf with a Chicago priest, Father John Nicola, an expert in demonology. So versed in this field is he that the producers of the movie "The Exorcist" used him as a top advisor. By means of many stories, sometimes told on vacation nights, he convinced us of the presence of satanic forces in our daily lives. His words, as they come back to me, drove us priests present to a greater faithfulness in our prayer life. Demons center their attacks on priests, the shepherds, he said. Judas Iscariot, a first priest, gave his heart over to the devils!

How well for all to know that evil spirits camp outside our homes! If they hear loud, angry voices coming from within—violent rages, violence in any form—they laugh and exult. This home is ready for a take-over by the angels from Hell. In the same way they, with their preternatural powers, lurk close to our hearts. When they see us taking chances with our purity of life, they let out a cry of anticipation and, like vultures, gather for the feast.

> *... because the mention of this Name sends the devils running for cover.*

Beware of over-confidence! If some say, "I'm too sophisticated to be affected by this risqué movie, this racy novel, or this dangerous friendship," they may be preparing themselves for a big fall. The more we acknowledge the weaknesses of our human nature, without despairing, the better chance we have to grow in holiness of life. We will throw ourselves on the Love of God for our daily strength. "Give us this day our daily bread."

Every act of kindness, honesty, truthfulness or decency makes our hearts, our homes, our community and our world a better place, less in control of the evil angels from Hell. I keep the Name of Jesus on my lips throughout the day because the mention of this Name sends the devils running for cover. They scream in agony as they hear It. I remember the words of St. Paul. "Pray for me, lest when I have preached to others, I myself may become a castaway."

A five-second decision can put us on the road to self-destruction . . . an intoxicated man decides to drive home. Crash! Bang!

Enrich Prayer Life Through The Three Persons In God

A year ago, in early June, 1994, some 600 Chicago priests met together for four Convocation Days, a time for spiritual and social exercises, at Pheasant Run in nearby St. Charles, Illinois. I enjoyed the heart-warming Masses, the spiritual talks and the chance to meet many old friends. Also, I had the time to mend fences with some brother priests disenchanted, in the past, with my way of doing things. Notice I said "some"—not "all"—took to my approach for reconciliation. I must have really disturbed them in days gone by. Maybe better results in June, 1996.

One talk, by Bishop Untener of Saginaw, Michigan, has stayed with me through the whole past year. In speaking about prayer, this young Bishop said, "Refuse to let your prayer dead end in Jesus." I never heard this theme put in that way. Three months later, in September, 1994, at our International Airport Chaplains Meeting in London, England, a Jesuit priest preached eloquently on the same message: "Enrich your prayer life by praying to all Three Persons of the Trinity—

the Father, Son and Holy Spirit." I was delighted to hear this suggestion repeated in London, so far from St. Charles, Illinois.

After hearing Bishop Untener last June, 1994, I began to pray much more to the Father and the Holy Spirit—of course, not neglecting Jesus in the meantime. God, the Father, gives Beauty to all Creation and, especially, beauty to our souls. As we admire the magnificence of Nature, our hearts cry out. "If this marvelous world we live in is only a faint glimmer of the Beauty of the Father, what an interesting, creative Person He must be!" My prayer life has deepened in the past year, because I find myself asking the clouds, the sky, the stars, the flowers, the mountains, the streams and all creation to give glory to the Creator.

What an exciting and fulfilling happening we experience ...

Also the Holy Spirit has entered my prayer life, more than ever before than in years gone by. I picture This Spirit as a Young Person—a Holy, Loving Person—deeply concerned with my life. How powerful and willing is This Good Friend Who can do unbelievable things in my soul!

According to Bishop Untener and the Jesuit priests in London, we can sum up the characteristics of Each of the Three Persons. The Father fills the world with

His trademarks of Order and Charm. Notice the faces of animals! We associate the Son with compassion, healing, forgiveness and caring. The Holy Spirit is aligned with every positive idea and inspiration that comes our way.

We can take more from life and give more to others if we, as individuals, share in the Trinity in our life of prayer. What an exciting and fulfilling happening we experience if we make the Father and the Spirit as familiar to ourselves as Jesus is!

The Sacred Heart of Christ

In my time in the Major Seminary at Mundelein, Illinois, a six-year stretch, we seminarians made the first Friday of each month a Day of Recollection in honor of the Sacred Heart. A blanket of stillness and peace fell over the campus as we students observed silence through the day until suppertime at 6:00 pm.

A Holy Hour in the Main Chapel finished off the Day of Prayer in honor of the Sacred Heart. At this last service, our Rector, Monsignor Hillenbrand, spoke of the attractiveness of the Person of Christ, His appealing qualities of kindness, gentleness and love. As the years went by the story of the Sacred Heart—His pleading for the love of His people—captured the hearts of all of us men.

I found the evening hours in my room the most difficult of the day. Every night of the school year, I had to be in my room at 7:15 pm and with no newspapers, radios or magazines allowed. We broke silence at breakfast the next morning. My little image of the Sacred Heart on my desk saved me from despair and the temptation to give up my efforts to be a priest. Every night, I poured out my heart to the Gentle

Christ looking at me with sympathy and understanding. Peace always came to me.

On Ordination Day, I consecrated my priesthood to the Sacred Heart. Since then, I have stood before hundreds of His statues and images to repeat those words of Consecration: I trust in you and I do everything for reparation to You, for my sins and the sins of the world; I believe in Your love for me. My chalice has a three-inch statuette of the Sacred Heart at the base of the stem. As I elevate the chalice at my daily Mass, my eyes rest on this Image of the One to Whom I have given my priesthood. This reminds me of my Consecration to the Sacred Heart. The Heart stands for the Whole Person.

> *... a God Who pleads for our love and trust ... oftentimes, He receives coldness and indifference.*

I was stationed for eleven years in the Parish of St. Margaret Mary, the messenger of the Sacred Heart. Was this a coincidence or was it a sign from the Lord that He was listening to my pleas for help to be patient, kind, forgiving and loving toward all? Here we have a God Who pleads for our love and trust, and sad to say, oftentimes, He receives coldness and indifference from His people.

Set up an Image of the Sacred Heart in your home.

Go before it in times of fear and despair as I did in the seminary.

A True View Of Life

About a year ago, I was driving west on 111th Street, on Chicago's South Side, with just enough time to make a 10:00 a.m. appointment. Suddenly, to my dismay, a red light came alive on my car's dashboard . . . the engine was overheating. Heat can damage a motor beyond repair, so I pulled into a nearby service station.

Told that the replacement of the old thermostat would take an hour, I felt exasperated and out of sorts. As I walked around the service station area to cool myself down, I glanced across the busy street to Holy Sepulcher Cemetery. Bells began to ring in my head. There, not 200 yards away, stood my family gravestone with the name "McKenna" on it.

My last resting place, next to my mother and father, lay in my sight with only the date of my death missing. What a change came over me, as a better perspective of life entered my mind. A short time from now, my body will be laid to rest in that grove of trees across the street. What importance will I give to this present car problem? I won't even think of it! A peace and calm entered my heart, as I spent the rest of the hour building up a new attitude toward the reversals of life.

How easily exasperated we become over the trivial happenings of life! Because of many stressful incidents, the motor of our inner spirit begins to overheat—with a consequent danger of burnout or a nervous breakdown taking place. We need a new spiritual thermostat, a fresh attitude which gives us a good perspective on life.

We need a new spiritual thermostat, a fresh attitude . . .

After the day of the overheated engine, I began to visualize my coffin being lowered into that plot of land, so close to the service station. At that time, few of the inconvenient happenings of life will have much weight. Missing short putts, meals overdone, my husband fifteen minutes late for supper—so what!

One day as I opened the refrigerator door, a plate fell to the floor. With utmost calm I picked up the ten pieces. My new attitude was working! How helpful for all of us to keep our final resting place in mind! When our inner motor begins to overheat from feelings of anger, fear, hatred, ill will, resentment, or impatience—we can bring peace to our heart by thinking of that ultimate destination. We can say to ourselves:

"My place of burial lies somewhere close."

Only one thing will have meaning: the love we have for God! As the Italians say so well: *Dio basta.* "God is enough." Joy is not in things. Joy is in us.

Interior of the great Notre Dame Cathedral.

The Holy Spirit:
A World Class Organist

Last week I wept as I listened to the background music of a movie entitled *Glory,* a story of a regiment of soldiers marching into certain death during the Civil War in 1862. I never weep over other things, not even my sins. Music has the power to bring out the best in our lives.

Notre Dame Cathedral in Paris, France, has the mightiest organ on the face of the earth. Because of its sophistication, only world class organists can play on this masterpiece of a musical instrument. Located on a high loft in the back of the Cathedral, the organ has five keyboards with 75 stops on each side of the keyboards. By means of these stops (knobs), the organist can bring in the sounds of all musical instruments: the violin, harp, clarinet, trumpet, French horn, flute and drums.

I have experienced some of the happiest moments of my life as I sat in Notre Dame Cathedral, listening to the glorious music pouring forth from this organ at the fingers of a world master organist. Like all others there on Sunday mornings, I felt lifted up to Heaven. God took on a new and exciting attractiveness as these thunderous, musical notes bounced off the walls of the splendid Gothic Cathedral. If God gave these musicians such talent to create this soul-stirring music, how Great must God be!

On this Pentecost Day, I can speak of the work of the Holy Spirit in my inner spirit, in my soul. I can look upon my soul as an organ, like the one mentioned above, a marvelous instrument which gives forth music to the world. The only Person suited to play on this masterpiece and produce its best is the Holy Spirit, the Spirit of Love!

I will find this music in the thoughts I think and in the words I speak.

Think of the complexity of the inner spirit, working through the brain with its 32 billion cells, its weight only three pounds. Part of the soul shows itself in the heart, the seat of all human emotions. How fragile and delicate these emotions, feelings, are! If I allow an unqualified person to play in my inner spirit, I will find second class, uninspiring music issuing forth from my life.

During these days of Pentecost, I'll listen to the music proceeding from my life. I will find this music in the thoughts I think and in the words I speak. Do I hear grunts, complaints, a loud, discordant voice, harsh words, hateful thoughts and sharp criticisms? If I do, I am allowing an amateur, unqualified person to play on the organ of my soul.

Invite the Holy Spirit each day to come and play glorious music in my inner spirit. Think of the beauty I can add to the world with this music of the Holy Spirit—loving words, spoken expressions of kindness and sympathetic charitable thoughts! I can make God pleasing and attractive to all in my presence.

A Crusade of Hope

Across our nation, youth have hit upon a daring program for bettering their lives in a Christ-like way. A few weeks ago, I saw a photo of a teenager with a band of cloth or plastic on his wrist. Inscribed on the thin band were the letters, WWJD. At first, I thought he was advertising some radio station, but the adjoining article in the newspaper told me the meaning of the letters: What Would Jesus Do?

In this simple way, young people are giving themselves encouragement to act as Christ would act in the many challenging situations they encounter. In all 50 states, groups of youngsters have formed clubs with this logo—WWJD—as their war cry. Many teenagers testify to the power and support found in this program. Instead of being confused and rattled by the awesome attractions to evil, they have this specific and concrete slogan before their eyes. What Would Jesus Do ?

With the benefit of their Christian education, adolescents know the story of Jesus of Nazareth. In the many difficult situations Jesus faced, He responded in ways easily understood by young people. He forgave people, condemned sin but not the sinner, acted courageously in the face of hatred and evil, respected women and spoke out for purity of mind and heart. WWJD—a wonderful way to grow in love and friendship for Christ.

Why cannot we older people do likewise? I am going to a friend of mine, a manufacturer of novelties, for a price on simple bands with the letters WWJD on them. If the cost is right, I will order a good quantity for the sake of those wishing to use them. If I only had such a reminder in past years of this ideal to act as Christ would, I would have avoided so many failures and poor judgements! In the exciting days ahead, my wristband with its call letters WWJD will catch my attention, reminding me to live out Christ's Life through my thoughts and actions.

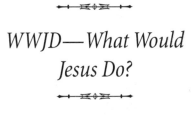

WWJD—What Would Jesus Do?

In my recent move to 9720 South Kedzie, Evergreen Park, Illinois 60805, an Afro-American man came to turn on the cable system. On his wrist he wore a thin, attractive, bright red band with the words: "Be Proud Of Your Heritage." Through the day, this message gave him inspiration and encouragement! In my seven-day stay in two hospitals in mid-April, I wore an identifying wristband, telling all my name and account number. My new wrist marker with its WWJD logo will lift me up to glorious, Christ-like ways of living!

Tell others about this new crusade sweeping the USA, a divinely inspired idea to bring Christ into our everyday life and thinking! WWJD—What Would Jesus Do? Give serious thought to becoming part of this wholesome, exciting March for a Better Way of Life.

The Bread Of Life

Lanciano, Italy. Sunday, April 20, 1997, 10:00 am. Our group of four arrives in this small town about 200 miles southeast of Rome. Back about AD 700, a miracle of the Eucharist took place in this community. After consecrating the bread and wine at Mass one morning, a priest had doubts about these elements becoming the Body and Blood of Christ. Suddenly, before his eyes, they turned into human flesh and blood. We have come to see these particles still preserved in a Church here in Lanciano.

In the Church we follow a long stream of people up a stairway behind the main altar to view this Eucharistic miracle. Just a foot away from my eye level, I see the Host and the Dried-Up Blood, both enclosed in glass. Through the years, many neutral experts have tested these remains and found chemicals and properties found in all human flesh and blood. Two Popes, John XXIII and John Paul II, have visited here in recent times.

Our party of four—myself, two lay men and a seminarian of 42 years of age—pray for a richer spirit of faith in the Holy Eucharist. On leaving Lanciano an hour later, we drive along in silence on our way to the town of Loreto, two hours distant, thinking deep thoughts about the Presence of Christ in the Eucharist. What a blessing beyond comprehension for all who have faith in the Words of Jesus at the Last Supper! "This is My Body. This is My Blood."

Back to the present. Every day, I bring the Holy Eucharist to an elderly friend, house bound, but with a keen intelligence. At the end of the prayers she always says, "Isn't this wonderful! What did I do to deserve this?" Her words have impacted me. I looked up the word "wonderful" in the dictionary. It gives four words: marvelous, extraordinary, astonishing, remarkable. No writer can find adequate words to extol the preciousness of the Gift of being able to receive the Body and Blood of Jesus of Nazareth into our hearts every day.

How blessed we are if we appreciate this gift … where the Holy Sacrament is kept!

Even after many years in the priesthood, I still thrill as I say those Sacred Words of Consecration in my daily Mass. "Take and eat. This is My Body. Take and drink. This is the Cup of My Blood." Miracle of Miracles! Only Jesus as God could have thought up this means of living in His people. Jesus, the Person of the Gospel stories, stays in our bodies for fifteen minutes after we receive the Holy Eucharist. It takes this time for the body to assimilate the elements of the bread and wine. What an excellent chance to share our life story with Him!

In the Blessed Sacrament, Our Gracious Lord makes Himself available for those wishing to pray in His Presence. How blessed we are if we appreciate this gift by often visiting a chapel or church where the Holy Sacrament is kept!

A Man Of The People

This past week, March 5, 1996, in the Holy Name Cathedral of Chicago, I attended the Consecration of a new auxiliary bishop for the archdiocese, John R. Manz, 51. I taught him first-year algebra in our minor seminary when he was a boy of 14 years of age.

During his 25 years of priesthood, Bishop John has always served in the Hispanic community of Chicago. He is probably the only Catholic bishop within 1000 miles with a moustache. Although of German heritage, he will now act as Bishop for the Hispanic Catholics of Chicago, under the leadership of Cardinal Bernardin. Over the years, his Spanish has reached an amazing degree of fluency.

Warm, personable, light-hearted—a true man of the people—Bishop Manz made a name for himself by reaching out to all in need of help. Usually the Holy Father chooses a bishop from priests in official positions in the archdiocese. In the case of Bishop Manz, he selected a humble, parish priest, one all wrapped up in the everyday lives of his parishioners. Not one to live in an ivory tower, our new bishop will launch himself into the nitty gritty of the lives of his expanded Hispanic community. He will walk among them with arms outstretched!

Jesus is this kind of person! Approachable, down-to-earth, in touch with the hardships of living—He met all peoples with words of gentleness. In the story where Jesus meets the Samaritan woman at Jacob's Well, we can marvel at His heart-warming approach to her problems. Her dissolute way of life had brought her despair about the future. Jesus offers the "living waters" of His Love, while showing her complete respect. He yearned to give her new hope.

We need the touch of the Master's hand to bring new life to our tired out, inner spirits.."

In his 25 years of priesthood, John Manz has brought the touch of the Master's hand to many people tired of living a life without purpose. I have spoken to many Hispanic people lifted up to a new faith in God because of the happy-go-lucky attitude of this loving priest, now a bishop.

After the Mass of Consecration, the new bishop spoke first at a slow speed in English. Then he burst into a sparkling flurry of Spanish, with a new fire in his voice. Frequent cheers sounded out in the Cathedral. His people, knowing his love for them, responded with an enthusiastic burst of affection for him.

We need the touch of the Master's hand to bring new life to our tired-out, inner spirits. Our feet drag with the boredom of living. We have tried many sources to taste a joy and excitement—some of them, wells of poisoned waters. In the past, we have ended up in blind alleys, distraught. Go to the well of "living waters!" Jesus, the Messiah, waits there for us!

In a recent survey, women desire kindness and gentleness in a man more than any other quality. Jesus has these qualities to the nth degree!

"Go In Peace and Joy To Serve The Lord And Each Other With Much Love!"

—Father George McKenna

About the Author

Father McKenna, the youngest son of Irish immigrants, spent the first 25 years of his priesthood as a teacher—first at Maryville Academy, then at Quigley Seminary. At Quigley, he was the spiritual director, guiding young high school seminarians in learning ways of righteousness and prayer. During the second half of his career, Father served as pastor and associate pastor at several parishes on the southwest side of Chicago. He also spent some time as a missionary in the Fairbanks [Alaska] diocese.

As Father neared retirement, he took on the challenge of establishing a chapel at Chicago's Midway Airport, which was experiencing a rebirth. Although *technically retired,* Father has now moved into his third career, ministering to air travelers and airport employees.

A lifelong resident of Chicago, Illinois, Father McKenna has been a world traveler, seeking inspiration across the globe. He has made twenty pilgrimages to Jerusalem. Father's favorite places to visit and write about are the Holy Land and Paris, France.

For fun, Father enjoys playing a good game of golf, especially with many of his fellow 295 retired priests in the Chicago area. He is the seven-time Senior Golf Champion of the Retired Priests of Chicago Archdiocese Association, having won their annual tournament each year he entered the competition.

On March 5, 1999, Father McKenna received the Archbishop James E. Quigley Distinguished Alumnus Award for special recognition and outstanding lifetime achievements.

After 55 years in the priesthood, Father continues to fulfill his life's mission of encouraging people everywhere to love God and others.

You may contact Father McKenna by writing to him (9720 S. Kedzie Avenue, Evergreen Park, IL 60805), sending him an e-mail (GMcK990103@aol.com) or visiting his page on the VCA Publishing website (www.govedic.com). He would love to hear from you.

Chicago Midway Airport Chapel
Mass Schedule

Saturday   **4:00 PM**   **Gate B-2***
Sunday   **8:30 AM**   **Gate B-2**
*Sometimes at B-12

- Services last one-half hour

- Father McKenna's homilies are only three minutes long.

- Confessions are heard upon request

- Communion is available before and after the Mass

- Free Care Notes® rosaries, prayer cards, and Catholic literature are available.

- Complimentary bulletin each weekend.

- Copies of Father's book may be purchased from the Chapel Volunteer Workers.

From the Publisher

Father George McKenna has brought godliness into our lives and the lives of many others. In fact, it was because his words evoked our hope and faith, that we were inspired to publish these small volumes.

If Father's messages have helped you in your life journey, or if they have transformed you in any way, we would like to hear about it. Please send us your story. If we publish your submission, you will be entitled to a free book and your name will be listed in the intentions for Mass at Midway Airport chapel.

Guidelines:

* The story should be true.

* It should not be more than five pages.

* For privacy you may change people's names.

* Focus on the uplifting power of Father's words.

* Be specific and stick to the point.

* Include "before" and "after" information about your life.

* Have fun writing it!

Recently, we began a program of placing Father McKenna's books in hotel and motel rooms. (Just like the Gideon Bibles) We feel that these books will give comfort, guidance, and inspiration to weary travelers. In order to carry out this plan we need your help. Please send your donation to the address below. Don't hesitate to contact us for more information about this wonderful project.

Mail your submission, inquiry or donation to:
VCA Publishing
P.O. 388352 • Chicago, IL 60638-8352

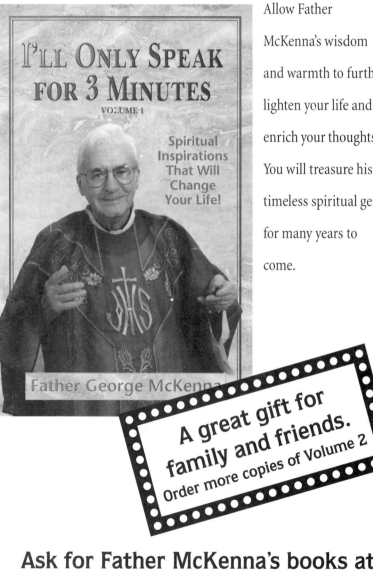

Also Available from VCA Publishing

Healing Others: A Practical Guide   Walter Weston

5x8 trade paper, 176 pages $11.95
Hampton Roads Publishing Company

The art of healing others through therapeutic prayer is not a skill limited to only a few people. It can be learned. Not simply theory or conjecture, this practical guide presents everything one needs to begin healing others, as told by a healer with more that 20 years extensive experience. Book one in a three-volume series.

Healing Yourself: A Practical Guide   Walter Weston

5x8 trade paper, 176 pages $11.95
Hampton Roads Publishing Company

Healing Yourself: A Practical Guide is the second of three volumes dealing with the theory and practice of healing. The same principles introduced in *Healing Others* can be applied to healing oneself. Here Weston provides everything one needs to begin self-healing through prayer. Book two in a three-volume series.

How Prayer Heals: A Scientific Approach   Walter Weston

5x8 trade paper, 256 pages $12.95
Hampton Roads Publishing Company

How Prayer Heals, the third of three volumes dealing with the theory and practice of healing, presents the science behind the art of healing through therapeutic prayer. People have been healing themselves and others for untold generations, but only recently has science discovered why therapeutic prayer works. Weston has over 20 years of extensive experience using prayer as an effective healing tool. *How Prayer Heals* is an insightful and revealing guide to the dynamics of faith and prayer. Book three in a three-volume series.

Three Volume Set (Regularly $36.85) **$35**

Order Form

Name _____

Address _____

City _____ ST _____ Zip _____

Quantity	Description	Price	Subtotal
	I'll Only Speak for 3 Minutes (Vol. 1)	$10.95	
	I'll Only Speak for 3 Minutes (Vol. 2)	$10.95	
	Healing Others	$11.95	
	Healing Yourself	$11.95	
	How Prayer Heals	$12.95	
	(3 vol. set) Healing Others, Healing Yourself, How Prayer Heals	$35.00	
		Subtotal	
	($4.00 for first book, $1.00 for each additional book) Shipping		
	Illinois residents add 8.75% Sales Tax		
		TOTAL	

Send check or money order to
VCA Publishing
Box 388352
Chicago, IL 60638-8352

You can also order these and other books from our web site at www.govedic.com

ORDER TOLL FREE **1-888-468-3342**